MW00812872

SCHOLASTIC

Follow the Directions... and Learn!

Dozens of Ready-to-Go Pages That Help Kids Learn to Follow Directions—and Connect With the Themes You Teach

BY PAMELA CHANKO

NEW YORK · TORONTO · LONDON · AUCKLAND · SYDNEY
MEXICO CITY · NEW DELHI · HONG KONG · BUENOS AIRES

Teaching
Resources

For Pete, who always helps
point me in the right direction.

Scholastic Inc. grants teachers permission to photocopy the reproducible pages from this book for classroom use. No other part of this publication may be reproduced in whole or in part, or stored in a retrieval system, or transmitted in any form or by any means, electronic, mechanical, photocopying, recording, or otherwise, without written permission of the publisher. For information regarding permission, write to Scholastic Inc., 557 Broadway, New York, NY 10012.

Cover and interior design by Holly Grundon
Cover and interior illustrations by Jane Dippold,
with additional illustrations by James Graham Hale

ISBN: 0-439-40071-6
Copyright © 2004 by Pamela Chanko
Published by Scholastic Inc.
All rights reserved.
Printed in the U.S.A.

2 3 4 5 6 7 8 9 10   40   11 10 09 08 07 06 05 04

Contents

Introduction

One of the most important skills for children to master in order to be successful at school is learning how to follow directions. For many children, preschool is the first experience in a group environment. Following directions is part of understanding how this classroom environment works, from lining up to doing an art project. School is a special kind of community, and getting to know its systems helps children feel like a productive part of that community.

Following directions not only helps children learn to work together, but also fosters independence. When children follow directions to complete even the smallest task successfully, it builds their confidence. Each success builds on the last, as children develop the skills necessary to become independent learners. Once children understand the framework of a given set of directions, they become free to proceed on their own with confidence. This confidence will help children as they move through the grades and tasks become more complex and sophisticated.

One increasingly important factor in children's success at school is their ability to perform well on tests. It is never too early to begin building the skills necessary for children to become confident test-takers. The activities in this book help children learn to follow oral directions, in addition to exposing them to written directions and visual clues. This exposure boosts children's performance in classroom activities—and prepares them for future homework and tests.

In this book, you'll find dozens of appealing reproducible pages that give children practice in following directions. They are easy to integrate into your curriculum because they focus on favorite themes—from weather and seasons to transportation. Engaging children in these activities also helps reinforce a variety of skills and concepts necessary for successful learning such as:

- alphabet recognition
- counting and numbers
- sorting and classifying
- colors

- shapes
- matching
- sequencing
- recognizing and creating patterns

For each theme, you'll also find activities that reinforce following directions, as well as book links to extend learning. The combination of these experiences enhances children's ability to follow step-by-step directions with accuracy and confidence—all of which adds up to learning success.

How to Use This Book

The activities in this book are organized by themes and designed to fit easily and smoothly into your existing curriculum. Look through the table of contents to find activities that tie into a particular topic of study, such as animals, transportation, school, food, weather, holidays, and more. For each theme, you'll find the following sections:

(About the Theme) A brief introduction to the theme, highlighting children's interests and experiences. This section also includes an extension idea, such as a whole-class bulletin board project, and book links.

(Activities) One to three activities in many curricular areas such as art, movement, language arts, social studies, and even cooking. These experiences are designed to give children practice in both following and giving directions as they play learning games and create interesting projects. The activities can be done as a class or in small groups.

(Student Reproducibles) Reproducible activity pages that can be used in a variety of ways to fit the needs of your class. Use the pages as a guided whole-class activity, in small groups, or in learning centers.

Supporting Students

Each activity sheet includes written directions in simple, direct language that is easy for children to understand. Read aloud the directions as children follow along with each step. You might copy the directions onto chart paper or sentence strips to reinforce one-to-one correspondence. The written directions also include rebus-style icons to support children's understanding. Before doing an activity, explain what the icons mean.

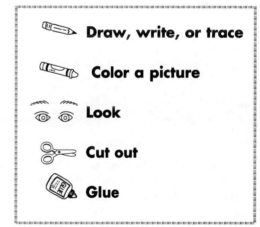

As you lead children through the activities, be sure to emphasize the correspondence between spoken and written words, and between written words and visual clues. This will help children become increasingly independent as they gain experience in interpreting and following step-by-step instructions. In addition, model the habits and strategies you use for following directions.

The themes and activities in this book can be done in any order. You might use them all or you might choose the ones that best suit the needs of your class. However you choose to use it, this book will provide you with a valuable resource for helping children learn how to follow directions, practice basic skills, and have fun in the process!

All About Me

About the Theme

One of the most exciting and fascinating topics for preschoolers to explore is themselves. Very young children are just beginning to recognize themselves as individuals, with personal attributes all their own. People come in all different shapes, sizes, and colors. They have different likes and dislikes. Young children are also delighted to discover their own bodies and what they can do with their hands, fingers, feet, and toes. In this theme, children will explore all the things that make them unique, from the color of their eyes to their favorite playground activities. Invite children to follow the directions to discover all the wonderful things that make up "Me!"

Extension Idea

All About Me Collages

Provide children with crayons, construction paper, and old magazines and invite them to create "All About Me" collages. Encourage children to look through the magazines and cut out pictures of their favorite things, such as favorite animals, sports, toys, and foods. Children can also draw pictures to represent different aspects of themselves, such as their pets, family members, and so on. You might even have children bring in photographs of themselves to include in the collage. Help children label their collages with their names and post them on a bulletin board. Invite them to describe their collages to the group and explain the significance of each item they included. You may want to do this activity at the beginning of the year, and use the collage bulletin board as a way to help children introduce themselves to the class.

Book Links

All by Myself by Mercer Mayer (Golden, 2001)
Look at all the things Little Critter can do by himself!

All I Am by Eileen Roe (Simon & Schuster, 1990)
A child explores his many roles—friend, neighbor, artist, daydreamer—to name a few!

Here Are My Hands by Bill Martin Jr. and John Archambault (Holt, 1987)
Read aloud these simple rhymes to teach about the parts of the body.

I Like Me! by Nancy Carlson (Viking, 1988)
A pig celebrates all the things she likes about herself, and shares some good habits, such as keeping herself clean, saving time for reading, and moving on after mistakes.

Olivia by Ian Falconer (Atheneum, 2000)
This playful book describes a day in the life of a high-energy preschool pig.

Simon Says

A great way to teach following directions while learning about body parts is by playing a game of Simon Says. Stand in front of the group and invite children to follow directions, such as "Simon says touch your toes," "Simon says rub your belly," and so on. Explain to children that they should follow the directions only when "Simon says." Once children are familiar with the game, invite them to take turns being the leader. Encourage them to use their own names in place of Simon, for instance, "Kayla says touch your ears."

Shape Self-Portraits

Provide children with precut construction paper shapes and invite them to follow your directions to make self-portraits. In advance, cut out ovals for faces (include colors to represent different skin tones), various colors of circles for eyes, triangles for noses, and rectangles for mouths. In addition, provide different colors of yarn for hair. Give children sheets of plain paper and glue. Then have them follow oral directions to create their self-portraits:

1. Find an oval shape. Glue it to the middle of the paper.

2. What color are your eyes? Choose two circles that match that color and glue them to the oval.

3. Find a triangle shape. Glue it underneath the circles to make your nose.

4. Choose a rectangle shape. Glue it underneath the triangle to make your mouth.

5. What color is your hair? Find some yarn that is the same color and glue it on top of the oval.

Who's the Leader?

An important part of following directions is learning to respond to visual cues. You can build this skill while exploring physical movement by playing a simple game. Sit children in a circle and tell them you are going to give them directions without using words. Invite them to follow a series of rhythmic movements, such as hand clapping, knee tapping, and so on. Tell them to watch closely as you change your movements, and have them try to change theirs at the same time as they follow along. Once children have practiced the skill, choose one child to be the "guesser." Have him or her leave the group as you silently choose a leader. Have the leader begin a series of movements as the group follows. Then have the guesser return to the group and sit in the middle of the circle. Encourage him or her to watch the group's movements carefully and try to guess who is giving the directions. Then it is the leader's turn to be the next guesser. Continue the game until each child has had a chance to be both a leader and a guesser.

My Senses

Your body has parts that help you see, smell, hear, touch, and taste.

① **Look** at the pictures.

② **Draw** lines to show which body part helps you do each activity.

Follow the Directions . . . and Learn!   Scholastic Teaching Resources

My Favorite Things

Mark which things you like best.

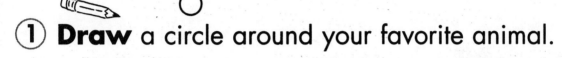

① **Draw** a circle around your favorite animal.

② **Draw** a square around your favorite activity.

③ **Draw** a triangle around your favorite food.

Scholastic Teaching Resources

Follow the Directions . . . and Learn!

Name _____

Let's Count

How many eyes do you count?
How many feet? How many fingers?

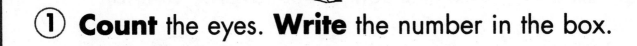

① **Count** the eyes. **Write** the number in the box.

② **Count** the feet. **Write** the number in the box.

③ **Count** the fingers. **Write** the number in the box.

Follow the Directions . . . and Learn!   Scholastic Teaching Resources

Name Game

Your name tells people who you are.

① **Draw** a circle around the first letter of your name.

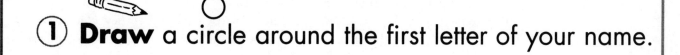

A   B   C   D   E   F   G   H   I

J   K   L   M   N   O   P   Q   R

S   T   U   V   W   X   Y   Z

② **Draw** something that begins with the first letter of your name.

Follow the Directions . . . and Learn!   Scholastic Teaching Resources

Friendship & Helping

About the Theme

Possibly the most important skill very young children learn in their first experiences at school is how to make friends. Preschoolers are just learning how to interact with one another by playing together, working together, and sharing. Children also build their self-esteem through helping one another. Young children are accustomed to needing help in completing everyday tasks; it can be a very exciting experience for them to be helpers themselves. When children participate in their new community by doing classroom jobs, they not only learn how to follow directions, but also gain a sense of accomplishment. Invite children to explore the concepts of friendship, helping, and sharing as you foster a sense of community in your classroom.

Extension Idea

Helping Hands

Create a bulletin board to track children's helpfulness in the classroom. Provide children with construction paper and crayons. Have children place one hand on the paper and trace the outline with a crayon. Help children cut out their hand shapes and label them with their names. (Alternatively, you might glue a small photo of each child to his or her hand shape.) Place the hands on a bulletin board and attach a sheet of plain paper underneath each one. Encourage children to watch for acts of friendship and caring in the classroom and help you list them underneath the helper's hand. For example, "Sophie helped Andres clean up the block corner," "Vincent shared his snack with Tanya," and so on. Update the bulletin board frequently, and encourage children to describe how it felt to help, and be helped by, their friends.

Book Links

The Best Friends Book by Todd Parr
(Little, Brown & Company, 2000)
How do friends treat one another? This book shows how friends are thoughtful, kind, and forgiving.

The Cleanup Surprise by Christine Loomis
(Scholastic, 1993)
A preschool class learns that one person's junk can become another person's treasure.

Friends! by Elaine Scott (Atheneum, 2000)
Children are invited to respond to various scenarios involving appropriate acts of friendship.

George and Martha by James Marshall
(Houghton Mifflin, 1972)
Two hippos' friendship survives and flourishes when they resolve conflicts together in five delightful short stories.

How Kind! by Mary Murphy (Candlewick, 2002)
One good deed brings another, and another, and another, all across the farm.

Friendship Beads

Help children practice both giving and following directions while making something for a friend. Provide them with lengths of yarn and beads of different colors and shapes. Pair children up and have them sit back to back. Invite one child in each pair to give the other directions as they string their beads on the yarn. For example, "First put on a blue round bead. Then put on a yellow square bead," and so on. Encourage children to give specific directions and listen carefully to one another—no peeking allowed! When children have finished stringing a length of beads, have them turn to face one another and compare their strings to see how closely they match. Then let children wear their matching friendship necklaces! Later, have children switch roles and play the game again.

Find-a-Friend

Help children practice following directions while pairing them up for special activities. Sit children in a circle so that they can all see one another. Begin by giving a child a "find-a-friend" clue such as "Find a friend who is wearing a green shirt." Have the child sit next to that person. Continue pairing children up with different clues, for example, "Find a friend who is wearing pink sneakers," and so on. Once each child has a partner, they can work together on a special project, such as making a picture together or doing a jigsaw puzzle. You can use the game to reinforce different concepts ("Find a friend whose name begins with a *T*") or to help children recognize special qualities in one another ("Find a friend who loves to jump rope!"). You can also use the game to help manage transition times. For example, as each child finds a friend, the pair can line up to go outside.

Show, Tell, and Teach!

One of the most wonderful aspects of making friends is that they can help you learn new things. Give children the opportunity to play "teacher" with their friends while learning new skills. Invite each child to think of something special he or she knows how to do, such as making a peanut butter sandwich, playing a certain game, and so on. Provide children with drawing paper and crayons and encourage them to draw step-by-step directions that show how to do the activity. They can also dictate directions for you to write next to each picture. Then let children take turns sharing their directions with the class. You might do a "project of the week," and have children take turns leading the group in a how-to activity.

Name _____

Cleanup Time

It's time to put away the blocks.

① **Cut out** the blocks at the bottom of the page.

② **Glue** each block on the shelf where it belongs.

③ **Color** the blocks.

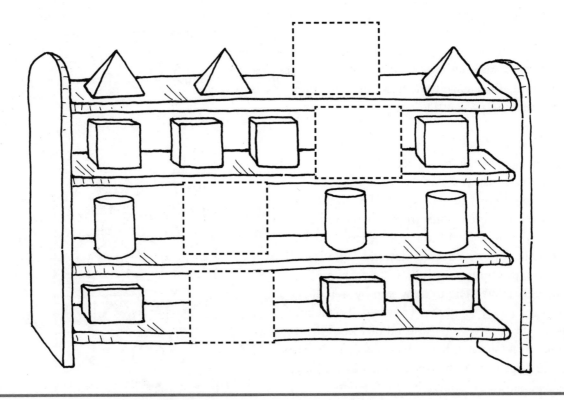

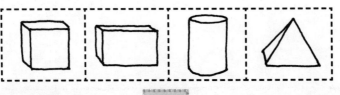

Follow the Directions . . . and Learn!   Scholastic Teaching Resources

A Perfect Present

What present is Ted giving to Jody?

① **Draw** a line connecting the letters from A to K.

② **Color** the picture.

Name _____

Who Can Help?

Friends help each other.

① **Look** at the pictures.

② **Draw** lines to show who can help each child.

Follow the Directions . . . and Learn!   Scholastic Teaching Resources

Sharing a Snack

Can you give each child the same number of cookies?

① **Cut** out the cookies.

② **Glue** the same number of cookies onto each plate.

Food

About the Theme

If there is one thing almost all preschoolers have in common, it's loving to eat! If you've ever noticed how the children in your class seem to liven up at snack time, you'll know why food is a favorite topic of exploration. Food brings people together, and is also a great way to learn about different cultures. Food is also a natural venue for exploring basic concepts, such as colors, shapes, and sizes. In this theme, children will explore the origin of different foods, create a class menu, and even learn how to follow a recipe. It's easy to make following directions fun by inviting children to explore their favorite treats along the way!

Extension Idea

Favorite Foods Menu Mural

Cut an oblong sheet of craft paper and write "Class Menu" across the top. Write the name of each child in your class in a column on the left side of the paper (or help children write their own names). Then have each child draw a picture of their favorite food next to their name. Post the menu on a wall or bulletin board and invite each child to name and describe the food they drew, and tell why they like it. Encourage children to talk about the taste, smell, and texture of their favorite food.

Book Links

Bread Bread Bread by Ann Morris (HarperCollins, 1989)
Discover how different people from different cultures prepare—and eat—the world's most popular food.

Everybody Cooks Rice by Norah Dooley (Carolrhoda, 1991)
While searching for her brother, a girl discovers that the families in her neighborhood—all of different cultural heritages—eat rice in one form or another.

This Is the Way We Eat Our Lunch: A Book About Children Around the World by Edith Baer (Scholastic, 1995)
This rhyming story takes readers on a lunch tour through several regions in the United States and around the world.

Zak's Lunch by Margie Palatini (Clarion, 1998)
A young boy lets his imagination run wild as he concocts the perfect lunch—but is it a great lunch after all or just a great big mess?

Rebus Recipe

What better way to teach following directions than by making a recipe together? Try the recipe below, or choose one of your own. Write the directions on chart paper and add rebus-style illustrations to show each step. When you're ready to cook, read the directions aloud with children, help them identify the ingredients, and have them take turns following the directions for each step. (Check with families about allergies and other dietary restrictions in advance.)

Soft Pretzels

1. Pour $1\frac{1}{2}$ cups of warm water into a mixing bowl.

2. Sprinkle in 1 package of yeast and stir until it looks soft.

3. Add 1 teaspoon of salt, 1 tablespoon of sugar, and 4 cups of flour.

4. Mix and knead the dough.

5. Take a piece of dough and make it into any shape you like. You might choose an animal or the first letter of your name.

6. Grease cookie sheets with butter.

7. Lay the pretzels on the sheets.

8. Beat one egg and brush the tops of the pretzels with it.

9. Sprinkle the pretzels with coarse salt.

10. Bake at 425 degrees for 12 to 15 minutes. Let the pretzels cool, and enjoy!

Name _____

My Menu

A menu shows the foods you can have at a restaurant.

① **Look** at the foods on the menu.

② **Draw** a circle around the foods you want.

Follow the Directions . . . and Learn! Scholastic Teaching Resources

Follow the Food!

Help the milk get from the farm to the boy's glass.

① **Draw** a line from the cow to the carton.

② **Draw** a line from the carton to the store.

③ **Draw** a line from the store to the boy.

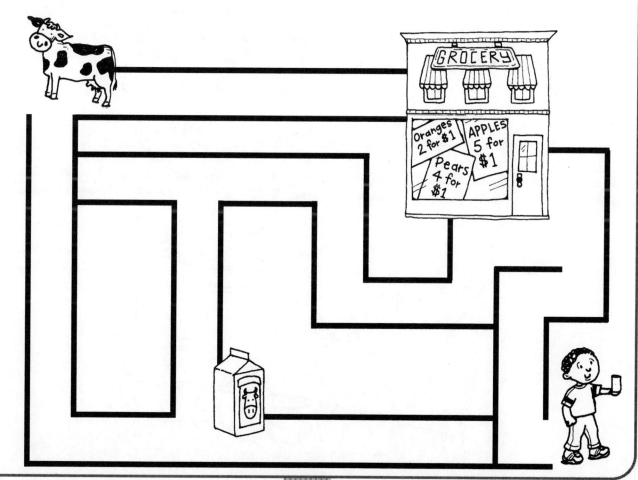

Scholastic Teaching Resources

Follow the Directions . . . and Learn!

Name _____

What's for Dessert?

What yummy treat is Lisa eating?

① **Draw** a line connecting the numbers from 1 to 10.

② **Draw** a line from the circle to Lisa's hand.

③ **Color** the treat red.

Follow the Directions . . . and Learn!   Scholastic Teaching Resources

Breakfast Foods

Different foods come from different places.

① **Look** at the pictures.

② **Draw** lines to match the foods with

where they came from.

Follow the Directions . . . and Learn!   Scholastic Teaching Resources

School

About the Theme

School can be a very exciting place for young children. There are new friends to make and a host of activities to explore. There are routines to master, from lining up to snack time and circle time. With so much to see and do, school can also seem overwhelming to some children. Learning about the environment of the classroom helps children acclimate and gain a sense of belonging. And as every teacher knows, one of the most important skills children need to learn to be successful at school is following directions! Practicing this skill not only helps keep the classroom running smoothly, but also helps children feel more secure in their new environment. In this theme, children will explore some of the activities, routines, and people that make up the wonderful experience of being at school.

Extension Idea

Who's Here? Activity Board

Invite children to create a bulletin board that helps track attendance as well as their favorite school activities. Provide children with drawing paper and crayons. Encourage them to choose a favorite activity they do at school, such as building with blocks, painting, dress-up, and so on. On one side of the paper, have children draw a picture of themselves doing the school activity. Help them label their pictures with their names and the word *school*. Then invite children to think of an activity they do at home, such as playing with a pet or eating dinner. Have children turn their papers over and draw a picture of themselves doing the home activity on that side of the paper. Help them label these pictures with their names and the word *home*. Post the drawings on a bulletin board with the home pictures facing up. As children arrive at school, have them turn their papers over so that the school picture faces up. During circle time, invite children to look at the board and figure out who is at school and who is at home.

Book Links

The Day the Teacher Went Bananas
by James Howe (Dutton, 1984)
A class is disappointed to learn that their fun, new teacher is actually a gorilla who has been sent to them by mistake!

First Day Jitters by Julie Danneberg
(Charlesbridge, 2000)
A twist on the age-old predicament—attending the first day at a new school. (Hint—it's the teacher who doesn't want to go!)

If You Take a Mouse to School by Laura Numeroff (Laura Geringer Books, 2002)
This tale chronicles an impulsive mouse's adventures in school.

School by Emily Arnold McCully
(HarperCollins, 1987)
In this wordless picture book, a young mouse decides to follow his eight older siblings to school. He soon discovers what all the excitement is about!

School Rules!

Classroom centers provide a natural venue for learning how to follow rules and directions. Each area has its own systems and routines. Divide the class into groups and give each group a large sheet of construction paper or tagboard. Invite each group to create a poster showing the rules and directions for a different center, such as the block corner, dramatic play area, art center, and so on. Help children get started by asking them what they do in each center. What are some directions they might give someone for how to work in the center? Also discuss special rules for the different centers, such as putting blocks away on the proper shelf, rinsing the paintbrushes, and so on. Then encourage children to work together to create pictures illustrating the rules for their center, and have them dictate sentences for you to write next to their pictures. When the posters are complete, hang them in the appropriate centers. When it's time to do an activity, encourage children to look at the posters and follow their directions!

Direction Detectives

Learning how to get around school can be a big challenge for young people. Make creating and following directions fun with this game. Gather a small group of children. Tell them that they will be creating directions for how to get to a certain place at school. Choose a destination, such as the lunchroom, water fountain, bathrooms, and so on. Then take the group on a walk to that destination, encouraging them to pay close attention to how they get there. Help them create specific directions as they go by counting their steps and pointing out landmarks. For instance: "Start at the classroom door. Take 12 steps straight ahead. Look for the red bulletin board. Walk that way for eight steps. Find the green door." Back in the classroom, write the directions on chart paper and invite children to create illustrations. Then have the group present their directions to the rest of the class. Can children guess where the directions will take them? Go on a class walk and follow the directions to find out! Work with a new group each day to create directions for a different secret destination. The rest of the class can work on a different activity to reinforce following directions with an aide or parent volunteer.

Time to Line Up!

Help the children line up to go outside.

① **Cut out** the children.

② **Glue** each child in the box

with the matching number.

1	2	3	4

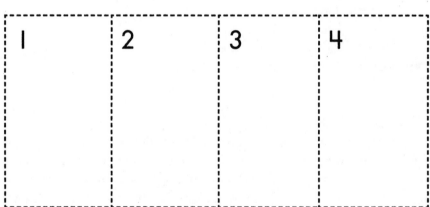

Where Does It Go?

Help put things away in the classroom.

① **Look** at the classroom.

② **Draw** lines to show where each thing goes.

Follow the Directions . . . and Learn!   Scholastic Teaching Resources

27

Guess and Count

How many things are in each group?

① **Look** at each picture quickly.

② **Guess** how many. **Write** the number.

③ **Count** how many. **Write** the number.

	My Guess	How Many

Follow the Directions . . . and Learn!   Scholastic Teaching Resources

What Do Teachers Do?

Teachers do many things at school.

① **Look** at the pictures.

② **Draw** a circle around the picture in each row

that does not show a teacher.

Weather & Seasons

About the Theme
Weather and seasons are the perfect topics for exploring science with young children. Whether it is hot, cold, cloudy, sunny, rainy, or snowy, exploring the weather always provides a rich subject for discussion and discovery. As each season comes and goes, children learn about the cyclical nature of weather. Studying seasons exposes children to the concept of climate. What is the weather like in winter where you live? What happens when spring arrives? Learning about weather also provides a natural opportunity for children to explore basic scientific concepts, such as change, and cause and effect. In this theme, children will explore different kinds of weather and the changes that come with each season. Curiosity is a natural motivator for learning basic skills—you can make following directions exciting and fun by tapping into children's natural interest in the world around them.

Extension Idea

A Tree for All Seasons
Invite children to create a bulletin board that changes with the seasons. Provide children with a sheet of craft paper, paints, and crayons and invite them to create a mural representing the current season. Encourage them to include the sky and ground. Ask them to think about what these things look like in that season, for example—is the sun bright? Are there grass and flowers on the ground? When the mural is complete, attach it to a bulletin board as a background. Next, invite children to help you trace the outline of a bare-branched tree on a sheet of brown tagboard and cut it out. Attach the tree to the background mural and ask children if they know what trees look like in that season. You might take a look outside to find out! Are there leaves on the trees? What color are they? Are there flowers or buds? Is there snow on the branches? Provide children with colored construction paper and encourage them to cut out shapes to represent what they see on the trees. Attach children's leaves (or icicles!) to the tree to complete the mural. As the seasons change, invite children to create a new background and make new cut-outs for the tree.

Book Links

Fall Is Not Easy by Marty Kelley
(Zino Press, 1998)
A tree tells why autumn is the most difficult season of all.

The Jacket I Wear in the Snow
by Shirley Neitzel (Greenwillow, 1989)
Rhyme and rebus add to the fun as a child dresses in layers for the snow.

The Snowy Day by Ezra Jack Keats (Viking, 1962)
Peter enjoys the simple pleasures of a snowy day.

The Wind Blew by Pat Hutchins
(Atheneum, 1974)
In this rhyming story, the wind snatches everything in its path—but will it change its mind before it goes out to sea?

Snipping Snowflakes

Invite children to create their own blizzard right in the classroom! Provide children with small, round paper plates, pencils, and safety scissors. Write the following directions on chart paper and include rebus-style illustrations. Help children follow the directions to make snowflakes. Display children's completed snowflakes and discuss how no two are alike—just like real snow.

How to Make a Snowflake

1. Place the plate on top of your paper.

2. Trace around the plate to make a circle.

3. Cut out the circle.

4. Fold the circle in half to make this shape.

5. Fold the paper in half again to make this shape.

6. Cut little pieces out of all three sides.

7. Unfold your paper.

Leaf Rubbing Matchup

Take children on a walk outside and encourage them to collect leaves of different shapes, sizes, and colors. (Alternatively, you can collect the leaves yourself and bring them in to class.) Give each child a few leaves, sheets of plain white paper, and different colored crayons. Have them follow your oral directions to create rubbings:

1. Choose a leaf.

2. Place a sheet of paper on top of it.

3. Find a crayon that matches the color of your leaf.

4. Hold the crayon on its side and rub it back and forth over the paper.

5. Stop when you see the shape of your leaf on the paper.

   Repeat the directions until each child has made two or three rubbings. Post children's rubbings on a bulletin board or classroom wall. Attach the real leaves in mixed-up order beneath the rubbings. Now challenge children to guess which leaf made each rubbing!

Snowman Shapes

Provide children with sheets of colored construction paper, glue, and the following precut shapes: small, medium, and large white circles; small black squares; and small orange triangles. Tell children that you will be giving them directions to follow, and that when they are done, they will see a snowy surprise! Have children follow these oral directions to make their snowmen:

1. Find a small white circle. Glue it near the top of your paper.

2. Find a medium-sized white circle. Glue it underneath the small circle.

3. Find a large white circle. Glue it underneath the medium circle.

4. Find two black squares. Glue them next to each other on the smallest circle.

5. Find an orange triangle. Glue it underneath the black squares.

When children have finished, encourage them to draw a snowy scene around their snowmen. They might also like to add additional features to their snowmen such as mouths, arms, scarves, and buttons. Post children's work on a wall of the classroom for a festive winter display.

The Rainbow Connection

Help children practice following visual directions as you reinforce colors and numbers with this activity. In advance, collect sheets of red, orange, yellow, green, blue, and purple construction paper. Mark each sheet with a number as follows: red – 1; orange – 2; yellow – 3; green – 4; blue – 5; purple – 6. Invite children to help you put the sheets in numerical order as you hang them in a row on a wall of the classroom. Provide children with plain drawing paper and red, orange, yellow, green, blue, and purple crayons. Encourage them to draw stripes on their paper with the matching crayons as you call out, "Color number 1, color number 2, color number 3," and so on. Tell them they should try to make the stripes touch one another as they draw. When children are finished, ask them to tell you what they see. They made a rainbow! For a fun extension, ask children what surprise they might like to find at the end of a rainbow, and have them draw it next to the stripes they made.

Name _____

What to Wear?

We wear different kinds of clothes for different weather.

① **Look** at the pictures.

② **Draw** a circle around the picture in each row that does not belong.

Follow the Directions . . . and Learn!   Scholastic Teaching Resources

Name _____

Snowflake Shapes

How many of each shape are in the snowflake?

☐

① **Count** the squares.

✏️

② **Write** the number. _____

△

③ **Count** the triangles.

✏️

④ **Write** the number. _____

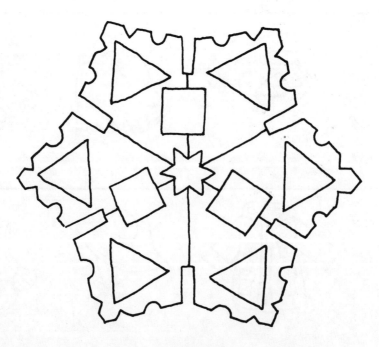

Follow the Directions . . . and Learn!   Scholastic Teaching Resources

Fun for Each Season

You can do different things in different seasons.

①👀 **Look** at the pictures.

②✏️ **Draw** lines to match the children with each season.

Scholastic Teaching Resources

Follow the Directions . . . and Learn!

Animals

About the Theme

Young children seem to have a natural affinity to animals. Children can identify with the animals in their world. Animals have families, just as they do. Animals come in different shapes and sizes, just as they do. Animals start as babies and grow into adults, just as they do. Whether they're furry, scaly, fuzzy, or feathery, animals are fascinating to preschoolers. Learning about animals is not only a wonderful way to engage children, but also provides a natural way to reinforce basic skills such as identifying colors and textures, sorting and classifying, and even counting. In this theme, children will explore their favorite furry friends, from the way they move to the noises they make. Invite children to follow directions from the zoo to the farm as they discover the wonderful world of animals!

Extension Idea

Who Lives Here?

Invite children to create a lift-the-flap bulletin board showing animals and their habitats. Begin with a discussion about where different animals live. Give children a few examples—for instance: a duck lives in a pond, a bird lives in a tree, a rabbit lives in a hole, and so on. Then invite children to tell about any animal habitats they know. Provide each child with crayons and two sheets of drawing paper. Encourage them to choose a favorite animal and draw a picture of it on one sheet. Then ask children where the animal they drew lives. Invite them to draw a picture of the habitat on the other sheet. Children may draw natural habitats, such as the examples above, or constructed habitats, such as a doghouse or a barn. Help children staple the top edges of their sheets together with the habitat pictures on top. Attach their work to a bulletin board and have them name and describe the different animal homes. Encourage children to guess which animal lives in each one. Then invite them to lift the flaps to see if their guesses were correct.

Book Links

Big Red Barn by Margaret Wise Brown
(HarperCollins, 1989)
Spend a day in the barnyard and explore the sounds of different animals.

Brown Bear, Brown Bear, What Do You See?
by Bill Martin Jr. and Eric Carle
(Henry Holt, 1992)
In this patterned book, each animal responds to "What do you see?" with the name of another animal.

Good Night, Gorilla by Peggy Rathmann
(Putnam, 1994)
The animals sneak out of their cages one by one as the watchman bids them goodnight.

Is Your Mama a Llama? by Deborah Guarino
(Scholastic, 1989)
A baby llama asks a diverse group of friends, "Is your Mama a llama?" Each responds with a rhyming clue, guiding the llama to guess the true identity of each friend's mother.

Animal Treats

Help children follow a recipe to make a yummy animal snack! In advance, use a round cookie cutter to make a circular piece of bread for each child. Provide children with paper plates, plastic knives, and the following ingredients:

- ◎ peanut butter
- ◎ raisins
- ◎ thinly sliced carrot sticks
- ◎ cheese slices cut into small triangles

Write the directions at right on chart paper and draw simple illustrations to show each step. Help children follow the recipe to make a kitten of a treat! (Be sure to check with families about allergies and other dietary restrictions before children eat their snacks.)

Duck, Duck . . . Horse!

Invite children to follow one another's movements as they play this variation on Duck, Duck, Goose. Sit children in a circle. Begin the game by walking around the circle, tapping each child on the head as you say "duck." Have them listen carefully for when you name a different animal. Then tap one child on the head as you say "horse." Invite the child to get up and follow you around the circle like a horse! When you sit down in the child's original spot, it is that child's turn to tap children's heads. Encourage children to name a different animal each time and follow the leader's movements around the circle. Continue until each child has had a chance to name and imitate an animal.

Kitten Snack

1. Spread peanut butter on the bread.

2. Add two raisins to make eyes.

3. Add another raisin to make a nose.

4. Add carrot sticks on each side to make whiskers.

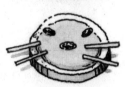

5. Place two cheese triangles on top to make ears.

6. Say "meow" and enjoy!

Name _____

Whose Baby Is This?

Help the baby animals find their mothers.

① **Look** at the pictures.

② **Draw** lines to match the babies with their mother.

Follow the Directions . . . and Learn!   Scholastic Teaching Resources

Name _____

Farm Count-Up

How many of each kind of animal do you see?

① **Count** each kind of animal.

② **Write** the number in the box.

Follow the Directions . . . and Learn!   Scholastic Teaching Resources

Name _____

Animal Homes

Help the animals find their homes.

① **Cut out** the animals.

② **Glue** each animal beside its home.

③ **Color** the pictures.

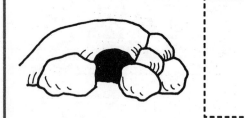

Follow the Directions . . . and Learn! Scholastic Teaching Resources

Name _____

Snake Pattern

Color the pattern on the snake.

 △ ① **Color** the triangles red.

 ○ ② **Color** the circles green.

 □ ③ **Color** the squares yellow.

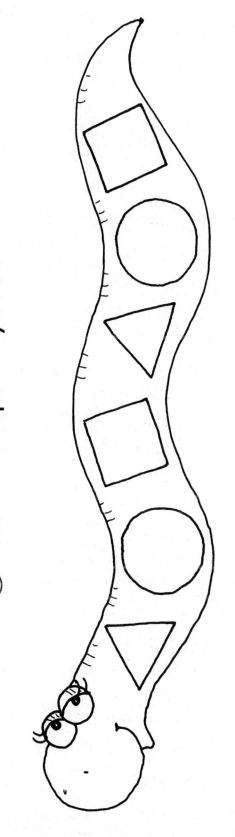

41

Things That Go

About the Theme

A favorite topic of exploration in early childhood is transportation. Young children are always on the move—they're walking, running, and full of energy. And they delight in learning about machines that go even faster than they do! Children enjoy learning how cars, trucks, airplanes, trains, and boats help people get from place to place and keep things moving in our busy world. Studying transportation also introduces children to different kinds of communities and helps them learn more about their own. Do the people in their neighborhood travel through city streets in buses and taxis, or drive on country roads in cars and trucks? Exploring different kinds of transportation can also help reinforce classification skills. Which vehicles travel on land? Which travel on water? And of course, one of the most important things to know when traveling from place to place is how to follow directions. Street signs and traffic lights help keep people safe and get them where they want to go. In this theme, children will explore all kinds of transportation. Invite them to get on board and follow the directions as they explore the exciting world of things that go!

Extension Idea

How We Get to School Graph

Invite children to create a bulletin board showing how they get to school each day. Begin by asking children to tell how they get to school each morning. Do they travel by school bus? Do they ride in a car or take a subway train? Or do they travel on their own two feet? Provide children with drawing paper and crayons and invite them to draw a picture of themselves traveling to school. Have them label their pictures with their names. Create simple pictures of various methods of transportation to use as column headings for the graph, and post them across the top of a bulletin board. Be sure to include all the methods of transportation used by the children in your class, such as bus, train, car, bicycle, walking, and so on. To create the graph, invite children up to the board and have them post their pictures under the form of transportation they use to get to school. When the graph is complete, discuss the results with the class.

Book Links

Freight Train by Donald Crews
(Greenwillow, 1978)
Train cars and colors are highlighted in this Caldecott-Honor book.

I Stink! by Kate and Jim McMullen
(Joanna Cotler, 2002)
A garbage truck makes its rounds while the city sleeps.

My Car by Byron Barton (Greenwillow, 2001)
Sam describes the parts of his car, as well as how he keeps it clean and how he obeys traffic laws while driving.

This Is the Way We Go to School by Edith Baer
(Scholastic, 1990)
This rhyming tale describes how children around the world travel to school.

Red Light, Green Light

Invite children to follow traffic signals as they play this traveling game. Begin by talking with children about traffic lights and the signals they give us: green means go, red means stop. It is very important for people to follow these directions carefully to stay safe. Create a starting line by putting masking tape on the floor. Have children line up horizontally on the line as you stand a short distance away. Show them two sheets of construction paper, red and green. Explain that when you hold up the "green light" it means they can move toward you. When you hold up the "red light" it means they must stop and freeze in place. Anyone who moves on a red light must go back to the starting line. The first child to reach you gets to be the next traffic director. As children become more familiar with the game, encourage them to try variations. Invite the traffic director to name a vehicle, and encourage children to move like that vehicle as they travel toward the traffic light.

Follow the Signs

Begin with a discussion about traffic signs. Explain that no matter how people travel, following these signs helps them stay safe and get where they need to go. Invite children to talk about any traffic signs they have seen, such as arrows, traffic lights, stop signs, and so on. You might even take a walk around the neighborhood to look for signs. Divide the class into small groups and provide them with construction paper and crayons. Encourage each group to work together to create a different traffic sign. If possible, provide children with pictures to guide them as they create their signs. (A good source is *I Read Signs* by Tana Hoban, Greenwillow, 1983.) You can also help them label their signs with the appropriate print. When children have finished, post their signs in various spots around the classroom to create a traveling route. Invite children to line up behind you as you lead them around the room. As you come to each sign, talk about what it means, and then help children follow the directions to get to the next sign. You can change the placement of the signs to create a different route to follow each day.

The Wheels on the Bus

Invite children to take an imaginary bus ride as they sing out directions for one another to follow. Set up chairs in short rows to create an imaginary bus, placing one chair at the front for the bus driver. (Alternatively, you can have children sit on the floor.) Begin by sitting in the driver's seat and practicing the song "The Wheels on the Bus" with children. Once they are familiar with the song, make up a verse for children to follow—for instance: "The children on the bus go clap, clap, clap" as you clap your hands three times. Encourage children to repeat the verse after you as they follow the movement directions. Next, choose a child to be the bus driver and invite him or her to create a new verse for the group to follow. Continue until each child has had a chance to be the driver and lead a verse.

Name _____

Air, Land, and Water

People can travel on air, land, or water.

① **Cut out** the pictures at the bottom of the page.

② **Glue** each picture where it belongs.

Follow the Directions . . . and Learn!   Scholastic Teaching Resources

Follow the Directions . . . and Learn!   Scholastic Teaching Resources

Name _____

Pattern Train

Choo-choo! Look at the pattern on this train.

 ① **Trace** a shape on each car to finish the pattern.

♡

 ② **Color** the hearts red.

△

 ③ **Color** the triangles yellow.

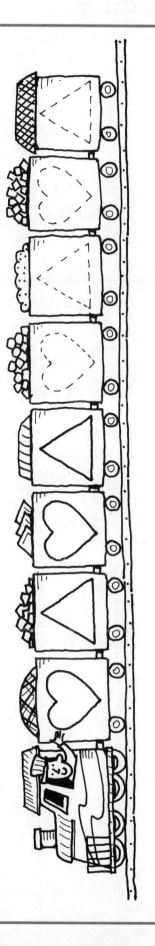

Name _____

Riding the Bus

Help the bus take the children home.

① **Draw** a line from 1 to 2.

② **Draw** a line from 2 to 3.

③ **Draw** a line from 3 to 4.

Follow the Directions . . . and Learn!   Scholastic Teaching Resources

Name _____

Colorful Cars

Cars come in different colors.

① **Color** three cars red.

② **Color** two cars blue.

③ **Draw** a circle around the car carrying a dog.

Follow the Directions . . . and Learn!   Scholastic Teaching Resources

Around the Town

About the Theme

Neighborhoods and the people who live and work in them provide an excellent way to explore social studies with young children. Whether children live in the city, country, or a small town, every community has certain things in common. There are places to discover, such as the fire station, the library, and the grocery store. There are the people who help in the community, such as firefighters, police officers, mail carriers, and of course, teachers! Following directions is a skill that is naturally built into the study of community. People must follow directions to get from place to place, in addition to following directions given by community helpers and leaders. So invite children to take a trip around the town as they explore what makes a community work.

Extension Idea

Community Mural

Invite children to create a mural of the neighborhood around school. If possible, start by taking children on a walk around the neighborhood. What do they see? If going on a walk is not possible, ask children what kinds of things they see on the way to school each day. Cut a large sheet of craft paper and provide children with paints, crayons, and collage materials. Have children work in small groups to create different parts of the mural, such as the school building, the grocery store, and so on. When children have finished, ask them what kinds of people they see around the neighborhood. Are there crossing guards and mail carriers? Do most people walk, or drive in cars? Encourage children to draw the people of the neighborhood on the mural. Then ask children to choose their favorite place to visit in the neighborhood, such as the local park. Invite each child to draw him or herself in that place on the mural. Display the completed mural and encourage children to talk about the people and places they drew. Invite them to point themselves out on the mural and share why that place is special to them.

Book Links

City by Numbers by Stephen T. Johnson
(Viking, 1998)
In this clever follow-up to *Alphabet City*, numbers from 1 to 21 are found in cityscapes.

Grandpa's Corner Store by DyAnne DiSalvo-Ryan (HarperCollins, 2000)
Can Lucy help Grandpa save his local grocery store when a supermarket chain comes to town?

Guess Who? by Margaret Miller
(Greenwillow, 1994)
Patterned riddles offer four silly answer choices, followed by one correct response. Features full-color photographs.

On the Town: A Community Adventure
by Judith Caseley (Greenwillow, 2002)
Charlie and his mother see their community with fresh eyes when they observe their surroundings for Charlie's homework assignment.

What's My Job?

Gather pictures of various community workers, such as a firefighter, police officer, doctor, mail carrier, construction worker, and so on. Alternatively, you might have children draw their own pictures of neighborhood helpers. Spread out the pictures on a table and gather children together. Invite children to identify different workers by giving them directions to follow—for instance, "Point to the worker who uses a hose," "Show me the worker who helps you stay healthy," "Hold up the picture of the worker who makes deliveries," and so on. When children are familiar with different ways to describe the workers, invite them to make up their own clues for others to guess.

A Homey Snack

Invite children to create a neighborhood they can eat! Gather the following ingredients in advance: peanut butter, graham crackers (divided into squares), and short pretzel logs. Write the recipe below on chart paper, adding simple illustrations for each step. Provide children with paper plates, plastic knives, and the ingredients above. Have them work in small groups and help them follow the directions to make their snacks. (Be sure to check with families about food allergies and other dietary restrictions first.)

Snack Houses

1. Place a graham cracker on a plate.

2. Spread peanut butter on the cracker.

3. Dip a pretzel into the peanut butter.

4. Place the pretzel in one corner of the cracker.

   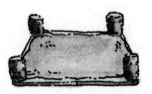

5. Dip three more pretzels into the peanut butter and place one in each corner.

6. Spread peanut butter on another cracker.

   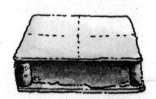

7. Place it on top of the pretzels with the peanut butter side down.

8. Dip one more pretzel into the peanut butter.

9. Stick it on the roof to make a chimney. Enjoy your snack shack!

Name _____

What Do They Use?

People use different things to do their jobs.

① **Look** at the pictures.

② **Draw** lines to match the workers

with the things they use.

Follow the Directions . . . and Learn!   Scholastic Teaching Resources

Name _____

In the Neighborhood

Can you find the numbers?

(1) **Draw** a circle around each number.

(2) **Color** the picture.

Follow the Directions . . . and Learn!   Scholastic Teaching Resources

51

What's Missing?

Things are missing in the neighborhood!

① **Cut out** the pictures at the bottom of the page.

② **Glue** each picture where it belongs.

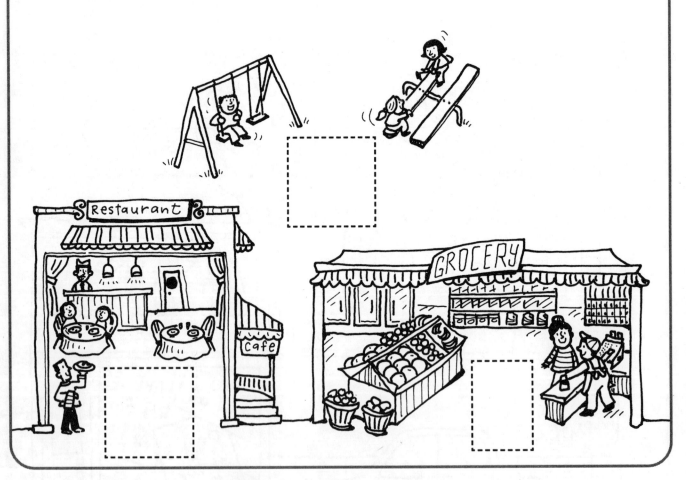

Follow the Directions . . . and Learn!   Scholastic Teaching Resources

Which Is Different?

One home in each row is not like the others.

① **Look** at the homes.

② **Draw** a circle around the home in each row

that does not match the others.

Follow the Directions . . . and Learn!   Scholastic Teaching Resources

53

Holidays

About the Theme

Studying holidays is a perfect way to teach children about different cultures and their traditions. Most likely, each child in your class has a favorite holiday and a special way of celebrating it with family and friends. The exploration of holidays allows children to discover the diversity in their classroom and beyond. The hands-on activities in this section help children explore several winter holidays, while the student reproducibles tie into Halloween, Thanksgiving, Valentine's Day, and Independence Day. You can make following directions fun by turning each lesson into a celebration!

Extension Idea

Holiday Quilt

Talk with children about the holidays they celebrate throughout the year. Encourage them to share what they do on these days, such as eating special foods, making decorations, and sending cards. Provide children with different colored squares of construction paper and crayons. Ask them what their favorite holiday is, and how they celebrate it. Invite children to draw a picture of what they do to celebrate that holiday on their square. Help them label their pictures with the name of the holiday. Attach children's squares to a bulletin board to make a holiday quilt. Encourage children to explain why the holiday they chose is special to them.

Book Links

Apple Pie 4th of July
by Janet S. Wong (Harcourt, 2002)
"No one wants Chinese food on the Fourth of July," a first-generation Chinese-American girl laments. But she learns that there's more to American culture than apple pie.

Hanukkah Lights, Hanukkah Nights
by Leslie Kimmelman (HarperCollins, 1992)
An extended family celebrates the eight nights of the Festival of Lights.

K Is for Kwanzaa: A Kwanzaa Alphabet Book
by Juwanda G. Ford (Cartwheel, 1997)
An alphabetic format is used to teach about a traditional Kwanzaa celebration.

Lion Dancer: Ernie Wan's Chinese New Year
by Kate Waters and Madeline Slovenz-Low (Scholastic, 1990)
A young boy describes his family's celebration of the lunar New Year.

Little Mouse's Big Valentine
by Thacher Hurd (Harper, 1990)
Little Mouse finally finds someone special who will accept his great big Valentine.

Thanksgiving at the Tappletons'
by Eileen Spinelli (HarperCollins, 1992)
A family learns that Thanksgiving is as much a celebration of family as it is of food.

Too Many Tamales
by Gary Soto (Putnam, 1993)
Young Maria accidentally kneads her mother's diamond ring into the family's Christmas tamales.

Handy Menorah

The menorah is a special symbol of Hanukkah. A candle is lit for each night of the holiday. Provide children with drawing paper, crayons, glue, and precut flame shapes made from orange or yellow construction paper. Have children work in pairs, assigning each child with the number 1 or 2. Then have children follow your oral directions to make their menorahs:

1. Partner number 1, place both hands on the paper so that your thumbs touch.

2. Partner number 2, trace around your partner's hands with a crayon.

3. Partner number 1, draw a line across the bottom of the outline of your hands.

4. Work together to color in each of the finger outlines to make candles. You should have eight long candles and one short candle in the middle where your thumbs were.

5. It's time to light the candles! Glue one flame shape on top of each candle.

Shape Christmas Trees

People all over the world decorate trees to celebrate Christmas. Give children practice in identifying shapes and following oral directions as they create a holiday display. In advance, cut the following shapes from colored construction paper: small, medium, and large green triangles; yellow stars; and brown squares. Provide children with sheets of construction paper and glue, and have them follow these directions to create their trees:

1. Find a small green triangle. Glue it near the top of your paper.

2. Find a medium green triangle. Glue it under the small triangle.

3. Find a large green triangle. Glue it under the medium triangle.

4. Find a brown square. Glue it under the large triangle.

5. Find a yellow star. Glue it on top of the smallest triangle.

When children's trees are complete, invite them to use yarn, glitter, and other collage materials to decorate them. Post children's work on a bulletin board or wall for a display of Christmas cheer.

Kwanzaa Place Mats

One part of the Kwanzaa celebration is a *mkeka*, a traditional woven mat that is placed on the holiday table. The colors of the mat are usually red, green, and black, the same colors as the African-American flag. Children can approximate a woven design using plain drawing paper, red, green, and black crayons, and a Popsicle stick. Hand out the materials and have children follow these directions:

1. Start at the left side of the paper. Draw a thick stripe with a red crayon.

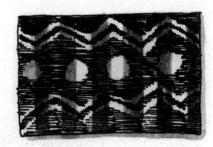

2. Draw a thick green stripe next to the red stripe. Try to make the stripes touch.

3. Draw another red stripe next to the green stripe.

4. Continue the pattern of red and green stripes until you reach the end of the paper.

5. Use the side of a black crayon to color the whole sheet of paper. Try to cover all of the stripes.

6. Pick up a Popsicle stick and hold it like a pencil. Use the stick to scratch a pattern in the black crayon. What colors do you see coming through?

When children have finished, you might want to laminate the mats or cover them with clear contact paper. Let children use their mats for holiday snack times.

A Red-Letter Day

A traditional gift for Chinese New Year is a special red envelope filled with money, for luck in the coming year. Invite children to participate in a variation on this custom as they follow visual cues and practice letter recognition. Provide children with envelopes, drawing paper, and crayons. Explain that they will be making a gift for a secret friend. Invite children to draw a picture as a gift, and place it in the envelope. Have them color the envelopes red. Assign children each a letter of the alphabet and help them mark it on the envelope. When children have gone home for the day, randomly place sticky notes marked with corresponding letters of the alphabet in children's cubbies. When children arrive at school the next day, have them deliver their envelopes by matching the letters on their envelopes to the letters in the cubbies. Then let children open their holiday gifts and guess who sent them!

Halloween Treats

Count each kind of candy.

① **Color** a box in the graph for each gumdrop.

② **Color** a box in the graph for each lollipop.

③ **Color** a box in the graph for each peppermint.

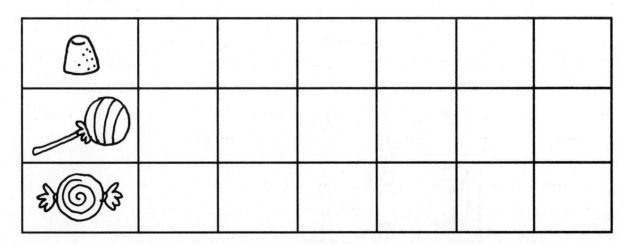

Name _____

A Thanksgiving Feast

Set the table for Thanksgiving dinner.

① **Cut out** the pictures at the bottom of the page.

② **Glue** each item on the table where it belongs.

Follow the Directions . . . and Learn!   Scholastic Teaching Resources

Be My Valentine

Deliver the valentines!
Each one matches a pattern on a mailbox.

(1) **Look** at the pictures.

(2) **Draw** lines to match each valentine

with the right mailbox.

Scholastic Teaching Resources

Follow the Directions . . . and Learn!

Name _____

Happy Fourth of July!

Do you see the pattern in this parade?

 ① **Cut out** the pictures in the boxes.

 ② **Glue** the pictures to finish the pattern.

Follow the Directions . . . and Learn!   Scholastic Teaching Resources

Health & Safety

About the Theme

Health and safety are extremely important topics in early childhood. It's never too early to learn how to stay healthy, from eating right to brushing your teeth. Practicing healthy habits at a young age not only helps children grow to be strong, healthy adults, but also helps them to keep these habits throughout their lives. Young children also gain more independence as they grow. This makes learning about safety a must in every classroom, from staying in line to learning how to stop, drop, and roll. Every child is fascinated by the idea of getting to be "big." Children's excitement about growing up creates a natural motivator for learning how to stay healthy and safe. And of course, staying healthy and safe involves learning how to follow rules and directions! In this theme, children will discover the importance of following directions as they begin their journey on the road to growing up.

Extension Idea

Food Groups Mural

Invite children to create a mural that shows how to eat right. Begin with a discussion about eating healthy foods. Explain to children that foods belong to different groups. In order to stay healthy and strong, people must eat foods from each group every day. There are certain foods people need to eat a lot of, such as fruits and vegetables. There are certain foods people should eat only once in a while, such as candy and sweets. Cut a sheet of craft paper into a large circle. Divide the circle into six pieces. Label each one with a food group: fruits; vegetables; milk and cheese; meat, dry beans, eggs, and nuts;

Book Links

Ah-Choo! by Margery Cuyler (Scholastic, 2002)
It starts as a simple sneeze—first the farmer, then his wife. Soon, even the farm animals are in bed with the flu!

Clifford the Firehouse Dog by Norman Bridwell (Scholastic, 1994)
While learning about fire safety, Clifford makes a heroic rescue.

Little Bear Brushes His Teeth by Jutta Langreuter (Millbrook, 1997)
In an effort to diffuse a daily struggle, Mama Bear describes the bacteria-based "battle" that will take place in Little Bear's mouth if he doesn't brush his teeth.

Officer Buckle and Gloria by Peggy Rathmann (Putnam, 1995)
Officer Buckle thinks the kids enjoy his school safety presentations, but the joke's on him when his canine companion steals the show. Winner of the Caldecott Medal.

Watch Out for Banana Peels and Other Important Sesame Street Safety Tips by Sarah Albee (Random House, 2000)
Officer Grover and Safety Deputy Elmo share safety tips.

breads and grains; and fats and sweets. Provide children with old magazines and scissors and invite them to cut out pictures of different foods. Children might also like to draw their own pictures of favorite foods. When children have gathered a wide assortment of pictures, help them place their foods in the appropriate sections of the display. Display the completed chart on a wall or bulletin board (you might want to choose an area close to the snack table). Encourage children to point out their pictures on the chart and tell what group the food belongs to.

Activities

Safety Signs

Invite children to help create signs promoting health and safety in the classroom. Talk about things they do and rules they follow at school each day that help keep them safe and healthy, such as washing their hands before snack time, being careful with scissors, lining up quietly for fire drills, and so on. Gather several sheets of tagboard or construction paper and markers or crayons. Divide the class into small groups. Encourage each group to create a sign showing health and safety directions to follow for a different area of the classroom. For example, one group could create a sign to hang over the sink showing how to wash hands; another group might create a sign to hang near the door showing how to line up. Encourage children to draw pictures showing each step, and have them dictate sentences for you to write next to the pictures. Hang the signs in appropriate areas of the classroom and encourage children to follow the directions they created.

Stop, Drop, and Roll

Invite children to practice an important fire safety technique as they follow visual and oral cues. Begin by explaining to children what they should do if their clothes ever catch on fire: stop where they are, drop to the ground and cover their face with their hands, and roll back and forth until the fire is out. With children's help, create three simple signs labeled with each step and glue them to Popsicle sticks. Gather children together and invite them to follow the signs and your oral directions as you hold up one sign at a time and call out "Stop, drop, and roll!" Once children are familiar with the technique, invite one child to hold up the signs and call out the directions for the rest of the group to follow.

Fun With Food Groups

People need to eat foods from different food groups.

① **Cut out** the pictures at the bottom of the page.

② **Glue** each picture where it belongs.

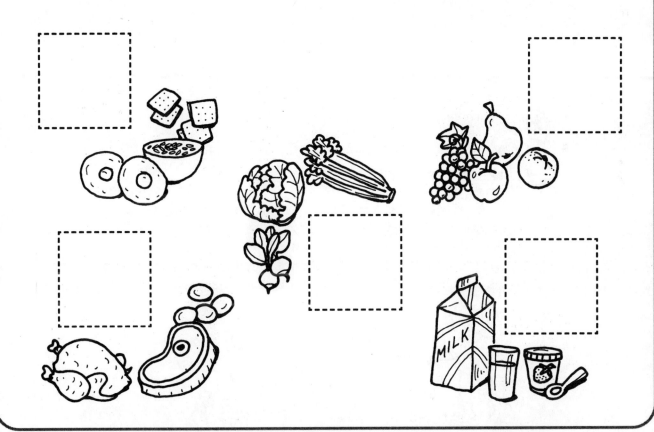

Follow the Directions . . . and Learn!   Scholastic Teaching Resources

Name _____

Safety First!

Everyone must follow rules to stay safe.

① **Look** at the pictures.

② **Draw** a circle around the child in each row who is being safe.

Follow the Directions . . . and Learn! Scholastic Teaching Resources